Flavours of Wales

THE CHEESE COOKBOOK

Gilli Davies and Huw Jones

GRAFFEG

The Cheese Cookbook
Published in Great Britain in 2017 by
Graffeg Limited

Text by Gilli Davies copyright © 2017.
Photographs by Huw Jones copyright © 2017.
Food styling by Paul Lane.
Designed and produced by Graffeg Limited
copyright © 2017.

Graffeg Limited, 24 Stradey Park Business
Centre, Mwrwg Road, Llangennech, Llanelli,
Carmarthenshire SA14 8YP Wales UK
Tel 01554 824000 www.graffeg.com

Gilli Davies is hereby identified as the author of
this work in accordance with section 77 of the
Copyrights, Designs and Patents Act 1988.

A CIP Catalogue record for this book is
available from the British Library.

ISBN 9781912050260

1 2 3 4 5 6 7 8 9

CONTENTS

Welsh Cheese

Any visitor to Wales will know that it is a land of green pastures. Perfect for grazing. Perfect for cows, sheep and goats to produce milk.

This is why Wales produces a plethora of the most delicious cheeses.

Although cheesemaking died out on the Welsh farms during the last war, due to the greater demand for milk, in the mid-1980s artisan cheesemaking really got into its stride.

Today there are at least 23 cheese producers in Wales, with some 136 varieties on offer.

With cheese producers from Pembrokeshire to Anglesey, some are large industrial sites, some are run as farmers' cooperatives and others produce artisan cheeses on farms.

The best way to find Welsh cheeses is to visit a good delicatessen or food outlet, such as Llwynhelyg Farm Shop near Cardigan, where you will be able to taste a selection of what Wales has to offer.

Here are some cheeses to look out for:

Abergavenny Fine Food
The original soft goat's cheese, Pantysgawn, has been made by the Craske family since 1981, and is now joined by a range of flavoured cheeses including goat's cheese with cranberries and goat's cheese with herbs.

Bodnant Dairy, Conwy

The dairy use local, pasteurised Fresian cow milk to create the Aber (Welsh for estuary) range of traditional, cloth-bound farmhouse cheeses. They include Aberwen (white), Abergoch (red) and Abermwg (smoked). A Caerphilly cheese, made to the original recipe, is the latest addition to the range.

Blaenavon Cheese Co

This company produce a large range of wax-covered cheddars, with 15 different flavours from whisky and ginger to Christmas pudding. They also produce 4 goat's milk cheeses.

Caerfai Farm Organic Cheese, St Davids

This farm makes a classic organic cheddar, Caerphilly and a Caerphilly with leek and garlic.

Caws Cenarth, Cardigan

This is a family business started by Gwynfor and Thelma Adams in 1987. Thelma, a leading light in the renaissance of Welsh artisan cheesemaking, now allows son Carwyn to run the business and indulge his passion for creating new cheeses. Caws Cenarth is the oldest established producer of Welsh Farmhouse

Caerphilly, with a range of flavours and new cheeses, including the brie-like Perl Wen, the creamy blue Perl Las and Golden Cenarth, a washed-rind cheese with a powerful flavour.

Castell Gwyn Cheese, Llandudno

Jackie Whittaker, an enthusiastic newcomer to cheesemaking, has developed very successful Camembert-style cheeses, Morwenna and St. Tudno, which is flavoured with sea salt and wild garlic.

Caws Mynydd Du, Talgarth

This cheese, the name of which means Black Mountains Cheese, is a traditional farmhouse ewe's milk cheese made by Andrew and Helen Meredith. They make it on their small family farm which nestles at the food of the Black Mountains to the east of the Brecon Beacons National Park. The sheep are mainly Poll Dorset and Poll Dorset X, and are fed purely on grass and crops grown and harvested on the farm.

Caws Rhydydelyn, Pentraeth

Menai Jones and Elin Wyn Jones make Anglesey Blue, Caws Caled, smoked Caws Caled and Caws Rhydydelyn. They also produce a cheese with local samphire, when in season, and run regular cheesemaking courses in Anglesey and Cardiff.

Calon Wen, Narbeth

This is a farmers' co-operative of 18 organic family farms, producing organic mellow cheddar and extra mature cheddar, with some exciting new cheeses in development.

Cosyn Cymru, Bethesda

A relative newcomer to the cheese makers of Wales, Carrie Rimes has had great success with her unpasteurised ewe's milk cheeses. Her cheeses include the hard-pressed Olwyn Farm, similar to a Manchego, Caws Chwaral, which is based on a slow-aging Caerphilly, and its younger brother Caws Calan. Her latest addition is Brefu Bach, a Chaource-like soft rind cheese.

Cothi Valley, Llandeilo

Here they produce a range of goat's cheeses to suit most palates. There is the fresh Luddesdown with added herbs, Caws Talley, white-rind Cynros or Arzegarzey and Diprose, which are a bit sharper. Their mature cheeses include Ranscombe, also available as an oak-smoked cheese, and the younger Storrington or delicious blue Talley Las.

Cwt Caws, Dulas

All Ffion and Nigel Jefferies' goat's milk cheeses are produced entirely by hand at Cors yr Odyn farm in Dulas, with the milk from a mixed herd of Sannen, Toggenburg and Alpine goats.

They make Peli Pabo, a soft goat's cheese available in plain, garlic and herb and chilli. They also make Ffetys, a salad feta-style cheese, and Môn Wen, a Camembert-style cheese. Their hard cheeses include creamy Seiriol Wyn, Cybi Melyn, Parys and Taid, which is a seasonal, extra-mature cheese.

Carmarthenshire Cheese Company Ltd

Steve and Sian Elin Peace, with their extensive dairy experience, started up in 2006. They make Pont Gâr, a range of soft-rind white, blue, smoked white, and white with garlic and herb cheeses. They also produce one of the original Welsh cheeses, Llangloffan, in white, red, smoked, and garlic and chive.

Glanbia

Glanbia are the leading mozzarella manufacturer in Europe. Their factory on Anglesey produces mountains of mozzarella, enough to cover pizzas all over Europe!

Dolwedd Farm, Cardigan

Nick and Wendy Holtham make ewe's milk cheeses. Their cheeses include Dolwen, a brie-style, Dol-Las, a blue creamy cheese, Fetys, a feta-style, and Beca, a hard cheese which won Supreme Champion at the Royak Welsh Show 2016.

Hafod, Lampeter

Becky and Patrick Holden produce Hafod, a traditional hard cheese handmade on Wales' longest certified organic dairy farm, Bwlchwernen Fawr. Created from the milk of 75 Ayrshire cows, the milk is left unpasteurised.

Little Welsh Cheese Company, Cymau

Jo Whittaker, owner of Little Welsh Cheese Company, runs Hope Mountain B&B. Her cheeses include a mature cheddar and a Gouda-style.

Merlin, Ystrad Meurig

Celebrating 30 years of cheesemaking, Gill Pateman and family now make 16 varieties of waxed cow's milk cheddars. They include King Arthur, a mature plain, Sir Galahad with rosemary and sun-dried tomatoes and seven varieties of goat's milk cheddar which are made to order.

Pant Mawr Farmhouse Cheeses, Clynderwen

Established in 1983, this family business is run by David, Cynthia and Jason Jennings at their small traditional Welsh hill farm located in the foothills of the Preseli Mountains. They make a range of cow's milk washed curd cheeses, including Caws Cerwyn, a hard, mellow cheese, also available in a smoked and mature variety. They also produce a soft Caws Preseli and a mead-washed Drewi Sand. Their goat's cheese offering is the plain Heb Enw or the smoked variety.

Sanclêr, St Clears

Elfyn Davies makes a range of smooth and creamy yoghurt cheeses on his farm at St Clears, with varieties flavoured with chives, and basil and garlic.

Snowdonia Cheese Company, Rhyl

Established in 2001, this award-winning cheese company make 10 varieties of cheddar: Beechwood Smoked, Ambermint, Ginger Spice, Bouncing Berry, Red Devil, Black Bomber, Pickle Power, Green Thunder, Ruby Mist and Red Storm.

South Caernarvon Creamery

A very successful farmer-owned cooperative with the Dragon Brand, milk is collected from 125 family-run farms in north and mid Wales. They produce Mild, Medium, Mature, Vintage Cheddar, Welsh Caerphilly, Vintage Cheddar with Leek, and Monterey Jack Cheddar.

Teifi Cheese, Llandysul

John and Patrice Savage-Ontswedder came to Wales from Holland in 1982 with dreams of organic farming. The combination of raw Welsh milk and Dutch expertise has produced a range of Gouda and Caerphilly type cheeses. These include their Teifi Goudas, featuring seaweed, cumin, nettle and garlic, their Caerphilly, and the highly-awarded, washed-rind Celtic Promise.

CAERPHILLY AND
LEEK PANCAKE DOME

Caerphilly is the cheese most associated with Wales and its mild flavour and pleasing crumbly texture make it a winner. This recipe makes a spectacular dish, suitable for vegetarians. However, with the addition of some cooked bacon in the filling, it will delight meat eaters too.

CAERPHILLY AND LEEK PANCAKE DOME

Ingredients

For the batter:

300ml milk

2 eggs

100g plain flour

1 tablespoon melted butter

Filling 1:

225g Caerphilly cheese, grated

125g bacon, diced and cooked until crisp

150ml double cream

Pinch of cayenne pepper

Filling 2:

1 large leek, chopped

100g field mushrooms, chopped

25g butter

Serves 4

1 Blend the batter ingredients and leave to settle for 30 minutes.

2 For the first filling, mix all but 50g of the grated cheese with the cream, cooked bacon and pepper. Then, for the second filling, fry the leek and mushrooms in the butter.

3 To make the pancakes, heat a small non-stick frying pan or omelette pan. Pour a tablespoon of batter into the pan and swirl around to cover the surface area. Cook over a gentle heat until bubbles appear on the surface, then turn the pancake over and cook for another minute. Make up 12 pancakes with the batter.

4 Layer the pancakes in an ovenproof dish, large enough to lay a pancake flat across the bottom, alternating the fillings between each later. Finish with a pancake on top.

5 Sprinkle over the remaining cheese.

6 Bake in a hot oven 220°C/425°F/Gas 7 for 15 minutes.

7 To serve, cut into wedges, like a cake.

CHICKEN WITH LEEK AND WELSH CHEESES

A tasty, quick and easy recipe that can be prepared ahead and popped into the oven later in the day. You can experiment with a variety of cheeses available to you, but if you are lucky enough to find some Welsh ones, so much the better.

CHICKEN WITH LEEK AND WELSH CHEESES

Ingredients

8 good sized chicken thighs, bones removed

1 small leek, washed and diced

50g chorizo, chopped

120g (4oz) Cwt Caws, soft, fresh goat's cheese

50g (2oz) Teifi cheese, or Gouda, cubed

Serves 4

1 Bone the chicken thighs, leaving the skin on.

2 Mix the leek with the chorizo, goat's cheese and Teifi.

3 Press half the stuffing under the skin of the chicken and the rest in the cavity left by the bone.

4 Arrange the thighs into neat parcels and put in a baking dish.

5 Roast for about 45 minutes at 200°C/400°F/ Gas 6.

ASPARAGUS AND ABERWEN PUFFS

Ingredients

450g asparagus, trimmed

100g Aberwen (or unpressed Cheshire type), grated

1 packet 375g pre-rolled puff pastry

25g melted butter

Salt and freshly ground black pepper

Serves 4

1. Heat the oven to 200°C/400°F/Gas 6.

2. Cut the pastry, across its width, into 4 long strips. Sprinkle the cheese over, leaving a small border around the edges. Arrange 4 spears of asparagus on top.

3. Brush copiously with melted butter and season well.

4. Bake for 10-15 minutes.

Aberwen is made at the Bodnant farm shop in north Wales. It is an unpressed, hard cheese like Cheshire. There are a number of excellent Welsh cheeses made by this principle.

PANTYSGAWN WITH MEDITERRANEAN SALSA

In 1981, Pam and Tony Craske made the move to Wales with visions of the 'good life' on a Welsh hill farm. Tony was sent to the local village market to buy a cow. Clearly something was lost in translation and Tony not only returned with a goat instead of a cow, but he returned with 6 of them. The family was soon awash with milk and unable to sell it, which led Pam to Abergavenny library where she borrowed a book on cheesemaking, and the rest, as they say, is history.

PANTYSGAWN WITH MEDITERRANEAN SALSA

Ingredients

225g Pantysgawn soft goat's cheese, cut into thin, even slices

6 firm tomatoes, seeded and finely diced

6 tablespoons olive oil

1 large garlic clove, crushed

20 black olives, stoned, chopped very fine

1 tablespoon white wine vinegar

1 tablespoon chopped parsley

1 tablespoon chopped chives

1 tin anchovy fillets, drained and chopped

Seasoning

Serves 4

1. Mix together the sliced tomatoes, olive oil, garlic, chopped olives, white wine vinegar, parsley, chives, anchovies and seasoning.

2. Spoon some of this salsa on to the middle of each serving plate.

3. Then layer the slices of Pantysgawn on top of the salsa, interspersing each layer with the salsa until you have a tower.

4. Sprinkle the remaining salsa around the plates.

5. Serve with warm malted bread.

OLYMPIC WELSH
CHEDDAR CHEESE
SCONES

This is a marvellous recipe given to me by a Croatian colleague when we were Games Makers together at the London Olympics. Their Croatian name is Pogača, and she said she makes up a batch when she is feeling homesick. Although this makes a great many little cheesy scones, I find that they freeze beautifully.

OLYMPIC WELSH CHEDDAR CHEESE SCONES

Ingredients

500g flour

250g butter

150g grated cheddar

1 x 7g packet dried yeast

2 teaspoons salt

2 whole eggs, separated

300ml sour cream

Sesame seeds

Makes 10-12 scones

① Mix the flour, butter, cheese, yeast and salt together.

② Stir in the 2 egg yolks and sour cream and mix to make a dough.

③ Leave the dough to rest for an hour, before rolling and cutting into discs.

④ Beat the egg whites to form a froth and brush on top, then scatter with sesame seeds.

⑤ Bake at 180°C/350°F/ Gas 4 for 15-20 minutes.

EWE'S CHEESE,
BEETROOT, APPLE AND
HAZELNUT SALAD

Wendy and Nick Holtham have a herd of dairy sheep on their farm, Dolwerdd Farm in Crymych, Pembrokeshire. Here they make four excellent ewe's milk cheeses, and the firmest, Dolwen, has all the characteristics to make a salad like this outstanding.

EWE'S CHEESE, BEETROOT, APPLE AND HAZELNUT SALAD

Ingredients

150g Dolwen, sliced and diced, if not too runny

Salad:

150g cooked beetroot

2 celery sticks

1-2 crisp, red-skinned apples

50g hazelnuts, toasted

Dressing:

3 tablespoons best quality extra-virgin olive oil

1 tablespoon fruit vinegar, raspberry if possible

Salt and pepper

½ teaspoon runny honey

Serves 4

❶ Chop all the ingredients for the salad into equal sized cubes.

❷ Scatter the salad over 4 serving plates and arrange the cheese on top.

❸ Mix and shake the ingredients for the dressing together until well combined and drizzle over the salad just before serving.

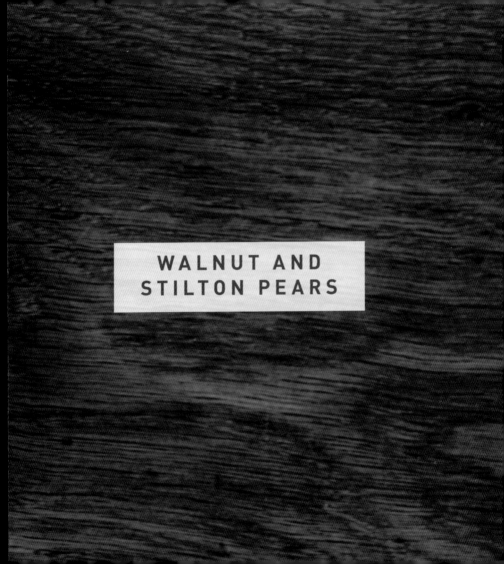

WALNUT AND
STILTON PEARS

Caws Cenarth creamery, first established by Thelma Adams with the introduction of milk quotas in the late 1980s, is still going strong, now run by her son, Carwyn. Although traditional Caerphilly is the mainstay of this creamery, new varieties of cheese are constantly being developed, and all to the same high standards set by Thelma. Perl Las is an elegant blue cheese, with lots of flavour and a creamy texture. Another blue cheese would also work well in this recipe.

WALNUT AND STILTON PEARS

Ingredients

4 large, ripe pears

100g Perl Las blue cheese, mashed

50g walnuts, chopped

A few whole walnuts for garnish

1 tablespoon mayonnaise

1 tablespoon brandy

Dressing:

3 tablespoons best quality extra-virgin olive oil

1 tablespoon red wine vinegar

½ teaspoon redcurrant jelly

Serves 4

1 Whisk or shake all the ingredients for the dressing in a sealed jar so that they are well combined.

2 Mix the cheese, walnuts, mayonnaise and brandy to make a paste.

3 Halve, peel and core the pears and press the stuffing into the cavity.

4 To serve, surround the pears with a spoonful of vinaigrette and walnuts to garnish.

CHEESY POTATOES

There is an abundance of excellent cheddar made in Wales. From Dragon cheddar in Pwllheli, Black Bomber by the Snowdonia Cheese company, Calon Wen in Pembrokeshire, or Hafod, which is a traditional hard cheese handmade on Wales' longest certified organic dairy farm, Bwlchwernen Fawr.

CHEESY POTATOES

Ingredients

1kg potatoes, peeled and diced into ¼ inch cubes

1 large pepper, deseeded and diced

1 large Spanish onion, peeled and diced

1 tablespoon flour

4 tablespoons chopped parsley

100g grated Hafod, or another Welsh cheddar type cheese

Salt, pepper and a pinch of cayenne

¼ pint hot milk

¼ pint double cream

2 tablespoons butter

Serves 4

1 Preheat the oven to 200°C/400°F/Gas 6.

2 Mix the diced potato with the pepper and onion.

3 Add some salt and black pepper, then sprinkle over the flour and add the parsley, seasoning and cheese.

4 Spread the mixture evenly in a 1.5 litre ovenproof dish, pour over the hot milk and cream, dot with butter and bake for 1 hour until the potatoes are soft, with a crisp topping.

GLAMORGAN SAUSAGES

Ingredients

150g fresh breadcrumbs

1 small leek, finely chopped

2 tablespoons laverbread

75g Caerphilly cheese, grated

1 tablespoon fresh parsley, chopped

Salt and freshly ground black pepper

Pinch of dry mustard

2 eggs, beaten

2 tablespoons light cooking oil

Makes 12 sausages

1 Mix together the breadcrumbs, leek, laverbread, cheese, parsley, seasoning and mustard.

2 Use the beaten eggs to bind the mixture together.

3 Divide into 12 portions and form into sausage shapes.

4 Fry the Glamorgan sausages in the oil, until crisp and golden brown on all sides.

These sausages, Wales' answer to the vegetarian sausage, are named after Glamorgan cheese which, at one time, was made from the milk of Glamorgan cows. It was made in the same style as a brined Caerphilly cheese.

CAERPHILLY CHEESE AND LEEK WELSH CAKES

Why not seek out an organic Caerphilly like Caerfai Cheese for this recipe? Caerfai is made in St Davids and has all the flavour and perfect texture a good traditional farmhouse Caerphilly should have.

CAERPHILLY CHEESE AND LEEK WELSH CAKES

Ingredients

1 medium leek, washed and shredded finely

50g Caerphilly cheese, grated

225g self-raising flour

50g butter

1 small egg, beaten

Makes 10-12 welsh cakes

① Dunk the leek in boiling water for 5 minutes, then rinse under the cold tap and squeeze dry.

② In a bowl, rub the butter into the flour until the mixture resembles breadcrumbs.

③ Stir in the cooled, cooked leek and grated cheese.

④ Add the beaten egg and mix to form a firm dough.

⑤ On a floured board, roll or pat out the mixture until about 1cm thick and cut into discs.

⑥ Heat a griddle or large frying pan to a medium heat and griddle gently until golden brown on both sides. Only grease the griddle if you think the Welsh cakes will stick.

Tip: serve warm with butter spread on top

METRIC AND IMPERIAL EQUIVALENTS

Weights	Solid
15g	½oz
25g	1oz
40g	1½oz
50g	1¾oz
75g	2¾oz
100g	3½oz
125g	4½oz
150g	5½oz
175g	6oz
200g	7oz
250g	9oz
300g	10½oz
400g	14oz
500g	1lb 2oz
1kg	2lb 4oz
1.5kg	3lb 5oz
2kg	4lb 8oz
3kg	6lb 8oz

Volume	Liquid
15ml	½ floz
30ml	1 floz
50ml	2 floz
100ml	3½ floz
125ml	4 floz
150ml	5 floz (¼ pint)
200ml	7 floz
250ml	9 floz
300ml	10 floz (½ pint)
400ml	14 floz
450ml	16 floz
500ml	18 floz
600ml	1 pint (20 floz)
1 litre	1¾ pints
1.2 litre	2 pints
1.5 litre	2¾ pints
2 litres	3½ pints
3 litres	5¼ pints

WELSH COOKBOOKS
GILLI DAVIES AND HUW JONES

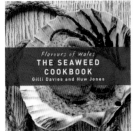

Gilli Davies celebrates the best of Welsh cooking and ingredients in her Flavours of Wales series of cookbooks.

Flavours of Wales Cookbooks make wonderful gifts at £6.99 each.

Available from all good bookshops, kitchen and gift shops and online.
www.graffeg.com Tel 01554 824000.

GRAFFEG
Books and Gifts from Wales

FLAVOURS OF WALES COLLECTION

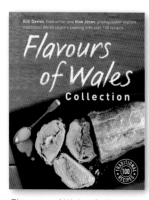

Flavours of Wales Collection book with over 100 recipes by Gilli Davies, photographed by Huw Jones **£20.00**

Cook up a Welsh feast with the full *Flavours of Wales* collection, in cookbooks, pocket books and notecards to share with friends.

10 Recipe Notecards and envelopes in a gift pack. Full recipe inside with space for a message **£8.99**

Flavours of Wales Collecti... in a gift slip case with 5 po... books **£12.99**

Flavours of Wales pocket books **£2.99**

Available from all good bookshops, kitchen and gift shops and online www.graffeg.com Tel 01554 824000.

GRAFFEG
Books and Gifts from Wa...